it is my heartfelt prayer
that you will indeed
find what you most
deeply want.

fr. joe

Betrayal and hurt and the desire for revenge are powerful emotions. It is a painful and difficult journey to find the courage and strength and heart to forgive. Fr. Joe has given us a way past, or rather, a way *through* this painful journey. In his usual pastoral style, he guides us slowly and tenderly to a place where authentic healing can find its way into our heart.

DAVID HAAS, *liturgical composer and author of That You Might Have Life: 12 Spiritual Practices to Nurture Your Call to Holiness*

Without this book, my parents would not have been at my daughter's First Communion. All I can say is, "Thank you!"

J.P., *business owner, St. Louis, MO*

The hurt in your heart may seem as fresh as it is old. You have tried to let it go, but you don't know how. This book will help. There is a way forward, a way of light and peace. Fr. Joe will guide your steps along the sure path of forgiveness.

FR. PAUL TURNER, *pastor, Cathedral of the Immaculate Conception, Kansas City, MO*

My mom was a tough person. I always loved her, but she also hurt me deeply. This book helped me feel less alone. I laughed and I cried and I will read this book again and again.

LISA, *St. Paul, MN*

In this powerful book Father Joe communicates the very heart of Jesus' message. The presence of God's love with us is expressed through his warmly empathic, totally down-to-earth style of writing. He shares practical, loving ways to deal with our painful hurts from others, from life itself, and from our own bad mistakes. Great touches of humor are interwoven with stories that bring tears to our eyes, encouraging us to trust that we can keep our joy alive. This book is a treasure.

PATRICIA LIVINGSTON, *Catholic speaker, writer, and retreat leader*

I felt SO understood when I read this book! No other book on forgiveness has ever done that for me. Fr. Joe truly gets it. I have already read this book three times. It's so easy to read; yet there's so much in it!

RACHEL, *retired nurse*

"Don't you dare forgive. Unless..."

FINDING WHAT YOU MOST DEEPLY WANT

Fr. Joe Kempf

TWENTY-THIRD PUBLICATIONS
twentythirdpublications.com

TWENTY-THIRD PUBLICATIONS
One Montauk Avenue, Suite 200
New London, CT 06320
(860) 437-3012 or (800) 321-0411
www.twentythirdpublications.com

Cover photo: Shutterstock.com / slhy

ISBN: 978-1-62785-513-6
Printed in the U.S.A.

 A division of Bayard, Inc.

CONTENTS

As I walked out the

door toward the gate

that would lead to my freedom,

I knew if I didn't leave

my bitterness and hatred behind,

I'd still be in prison.

NELSON MANDELA

INTRODUCTION

W hen the priest who tried to ruin my reputation and run me out of the parish went to jail, I knew that he could no longer hurt me or anyone else, at least for a while. There would come a day, I figured, when I would not cry as much. Sadly, however, I was afraid that I might never again feel the same joy for life I once did. That was what most broke my heart. To even think about forgiving at that time would not have made any sense.

Years have passed. Some of that pain will always be a part of me. Yet those wounds have little power over me now. I am so much more alive and free. Did forgiveness play a part?

Like you, I make my way through life as best as I can. Of course I've been hurt. No one ever said life would be fair. Sadly, I've also hurt people along the way.

Everyone suffers at the hands of others. Sometimes, the damage is awful. Why do so many people tell us it is important to forgive? What does that even mean? Are there steps to take to become more free? Does the pain ever get better?

From my vantage point as priest, I often see the wounds people carry. At the same time, I am often blessed to see folks who choose important and beautiful ways to deal with their pain. Watching that kind of goodness unfold is one of my life's greatest joys.

And so I offer these short essays, with a few stories, a few suggestions, a few thoughts on the way.

Clearly, I am not a scholar. In my heart, I am a pastor. It is from that perspective that I write: as family member and friend, as sinner and saint, as someone so much more like you than not.

Fr. Joe

Seriously.
Don't.

*My heart was broken and my head
was just barely inhabitable.*

ANNE LAMOTT

To this day, I don't know why the new pastor consistently lied about me or needed people to hate me. Nor did I have any explanation for why he kept changing locks in the rectory to give me less and less access in my own home. It was, however, when I saw him spit in my food when he thought no one was looking that I knew I would have to ask to be transferred.

Before I could do anything with that thought, I received a late-night phone call from a distraught parishioner. Evidently, at a small social gathering, this pastor put his hands down the pants of a thirteen-year-old boy.

Within the week, the archbishop removed the priest from the parish and asked me to say nothing during the period of investigation. That weekend, the pastor announced at all the Masses that he would be leaving the parish. To his circle of power in the parish he blamed his leaving on me. Between Masses, a number of people screamed at me for "what I had done to that poor man."

After the last Mass, I locked up the church and, exhausted, closed the rectory door behind me. For a while, I just stood there, leaning with my back against the door, trying to stop shaking.

Who knows how long I stood like that? The ring of the doorbell startled me, and I did not know if I should answer it. When I did, I opened the door to a woman who showed me a picture of marks on the face of her son. She said they were made by that pastor who had hit her child while he was serving Mass. Shortly after that, the doorbell rang again, this time by a man also angry at the harm this priest had done to one of his kids. Me? I mostly just wanted to cry. That is, until someone told me, "You just need to forgive." That is when I just wanted to scream.

No, I did NOT just need to forgive. What would that even mean? Why would anyone even think that was a good thing to say right then? At that moment, the suggestion that I should forgive felt like even more violence. Because it was.

No one has to tell you how you've been wronged. Maybe it's a small thing that still eats on you. Or perhaps the offenses were awful. Maybe just hearing that person's name gives you a pit in the stomach. Perhaps your anger wakes you in the middle of the night.

How many times do you or I replay that conversation or relive that scene? Often, many of us get angry at ourselves for not handling the situation differently. We wonder which parts might have been our own fault. For some, the hurt is shoved in our faces again each time we open the door, with every approaching holiday, or perhaps with each breath.

There is often a part of us that does not want to forget. Or, if we try to forget, even when we shove the memory of the pain as far down inside us as we can, there is usually some part of us that still knows it's there. For these offenses also touch into our core wounds.

Often our bodies also carry the effects of the hurts. There is data that shows the negative consequences of trauma and anger to our health—when we know it, and when we don't.

What do we do with all of our pain and hurt? Perhaps it is easier to say what *not* to do. One of the first things is to avoid telling ourselves we are not angry when we are. There is wisdom to this insight: "What we don't deal with will deal with us."

A friend of mine once told me: "I hated my uncle. He was a sexual molester. My grandmother kept him at bay, but the damage was done. I once heard myself say, 'I wouldn't care if a train hit him and drug him for miles down the track. I might even cheer it on.' I was told that perhaps I should work on forgiveness."

My thought for her? Yes, but perhaps not yet.

Though I want my friend to know the freedom and healing that come from forgiveness, we are often much too glib about what that means.

Unless...

*I've had a few arguments with people,
but I never carry a grudge. You know why?
While you're carrying a grudge,
they're out dancing.* **BUDDY HACKETT**

J esus told amazing stories. One of his best-known
begins this way:

> A man has two sons. The younger of them says to
> his father, "Father, give me the share of the estate
> that is coming to me." So the father divides up the
> property. Some days later this younger son collects
> all his belongings and goes off to a distant land,
> where he squanders his money on dissolute living.

If you do not know this story it is well worth reading.
It is often called the story of "The Prodigal Son" and
appears in the middle of Luke's gospel (Luke 15:11–32).
In this two-part story Jesus gives us some of the clearest
insight into his own heart.

Jesus invites us to meet a God more wonderful than
we had ever imagined, a God of truly unconditional forgiveness and extravagant love. I've long thought that if

we could only know one story about God and we knew this story, it would be enough.

Jesus makes one thing very clear: we do not have enough power to make God stop loving us. No matter how badly we've messed up, God is always inviting us home, waiting to welcome us again into loving arms. *This* is the God of Jesus.

Then, after this stunning story of a dad's astonishing love, Jesus turns us dramatically to the older brother. In the story of the prodigal son, it is pretty obvious that the prodigal son is lost. It is just as true that—in his anger—the elder brother is also lost.

And because the father loves this son just as much, he invites him home also, asking him to move beyond his hurt and anger at his younger brother. This too is the God of Jesus.

Many Scripture scholars tell us that forgiveness is the heart of the gospel, the clearest summary of the message of Jesus. We see Jesus forgive, and we hear his clarion call that we do the same.

Why is forgiveness so important to Jesus? It's simple: Jesus loves us so much that he wants us to be free! Jesus knows that if we want a joy-filled life, we have to take this road-less-traveled and do the hard work of forgiving.

And if we don't?

Some years ago, a man I know buried his daughter, the victim of a drunken driver who swerved into her lane and killed her. Several weeks after the funeral, we talked about what it felt like for him to try to go through life

without his daughter, taken from him in such a senseless act.

He talked about how food tasted like sawdust, how
it broke his heart to watch his other family members
grieve, and how lonely it was to watch the rest of the
world go on as if nothing had happened. At one point
he said, "This all seems like a dream, and I can hardly
imagine my life without her." He put his head down for
a while, and I wasn't sure what he was thinking. Then
he looked up at me and said, "I will have anger, but I will
not have hatred." He said, "If I have hatred in my heart,
that senseless act of violence claims another victim."

"If I have hatred in my heart, that senseless act of
violence claims another victim." This heartbroken man
knows a profound truth. There is a price to pay for *not*
forgiving. The smoldering anger of non-forgiveness will
cause great harm, whether we are aware of it or not.

Jesus knows we have all been wronged: Each of us—
in small ways or in big ways—has been treated unfairly,
taken advantage of, or harmed by some injustice. What
we choose to do with those wrongs will profoundly
affect the kind of person we are, the kind of life we have.

Most simply: forgiveness is not optional for those
who want a joy-filled, meaningful life. Forgiveness is
essential to our souls; it is the heart of truly holy and
happy living. To *not* forgive has been well described as
like drinking rat poison and then waiting for the rat to
die. The rat will be just fine, but we won't. Some part of
us dies.

We could try revenge, repression, or resentment, but only forgiveness breaks us open to a life of joy.

Through his life and even in his death, Jesus proclaimed that forgiveness is the path to life. I believe that all the holy women, children, and men who love us and have gone before us in death would also tell us that the work of forgiveness is worth it.

For when we forgive, we are not losing. We are setting ourselves free.

What forgiveness is *not*

Hope has two beautiful daughters;
their names are Anger and Courage.
Anger at the way things are,
and courage to ensure that
they do not remain as they are.

SAINT AUGUSTINE

R ecently, the daughter of one of our parishioners was shot to death while shopping at a religious goods store. When the police captured his daughter's murderer several days later, this parishioner told me how relieved he was.

This humble, good man said to me: "Quite honestly, Fr. Joe, I hope the man never gets out of prison because, if he does, my boys would probably want to kill him. Then I'd lose my sons as well." He added, "I don't expect them to forgive that man. Instead, I've been working with them to help them transition to something more positive."

"I don't expect them to forgive that man, but to transition to something more positive." That is precisely the stuff of forgiveness.

I wish we had a different word than *forgiveness*. Sadly, the word is a stumbling block for many because it has become laden with so many levels of misunderstanding. "Transitioning to something more positive" is a clumsy phrase, but it is a good description of the key energy that forgiveness is all about.

Too many people operate from the misconception that forgiveness means acting like no wrong was done. They fear that forgiveness implies that we are excusing the other's behavior, that we are somehow saying it was okay. No. If that's what forgiveness meant, of course we wouldn't forgive! Even if there might be extenuating circumstances, forgiveness does not mean we condone the wrong that was done to us or others.

A different misunderstanding about forgiveness is the fear that it means we have to remain in situations where we will be wronged again and again. No! We are not meant to live in abusive environments. Sometimes, abusers will use Jesus' call to forgiveness as a way to manipulate a vulnerable person into staying under their power. No! Sometimes, forgiveness means we need to step away from another.

It is also a delusion to think that revenge will help us on the path. Revenge is a false light; there is no life there. The death penalty is often the extreme example of our desire for revenge. The death penalty has been shown not to be a deterrent; it seems more to be a way for people to try to get some sort of satisfaction for the wrong done to them. But it does not appear to do that, either. The reactions of persons who watch the execution of those who killed their loved ones seems most commonly to be that it was "not enough." The death of the murderer did not quench their hurt. Something inside of ourselves dies when we seek revenge. Forgiveness includes working to willingly give up our desire for revenge.

It was maybe a year or so after that priest I had lived with went to jail that I decided to bring all that was inside me to the Sacrament of Reconciliation (often called Confession). This sacrament can be a healing place to take our sin and our brokenness, and I wanted to bring whatever was sinful on my part in all of this and to ask for the healing I needed.

When I told the priest, "For whatever was sinful about my anger, I am sorry," I heard myself quickly add, "but I am not sorry for most of that anger." Nor should I have been. For it was my anger, in part, that helped me do what was needed to stand up to this man so that less damage would be done. What he did was *not* okay.

There is a power in us...

I am not what happened to me.
I am what I choose to become.
CARL JUNG

An older fellow—with a postcard in his hand—approaches another customer writing at the post office desk. The old man says to him, "Young man, could you please address this postcard for me?" The young man gladly does so. He also agrees to write a short message and sign the card for the man. Finally, the younger man asks, "Is there anything else I can do for you?" The old man thinks about it for a moment and says, "Yes, at the end could you put 'PS. Please excuse the sloppy handwriting'?"

Why is it that some of us are more thankful than others? Why is it that some go through life with greater joy? The answer is not how many possessions we have, or how much we have suffered or have not suffered. It has everything to do with where we put our focus.

There are studies that indicate that only ten percent of our happiness depends on our circumstances. A certain percentage of our happiness is the baseline temperament with which we are born, but most of it has to do with attitude.

This is *not* to deny what is difficult about life. This is simply to remind us that we have choices. People can certainly cause us pain. People can harm us and those we love. But there is that which they cannot do. No one can take away our dignity; no one can take away our joy. We can choose to give those away, but no one can take them from us.

There is a power and goodness in us not diminished by the ways people treat us. We are truly more than our wounds.

Jesus never promised that life would be easy. Life is hard. Yet the good and the bad never cancel each other out. It has often been rightly said that life is both/and, not either/or. And we are wise when we choose to intentionally look at the blessings that are ours along the way.

Even in the midst of what is painful about life, the more we look for stuff to be grateful for, the more we'll see it. Because it is there. And the more we do that, the more we'll be able to draw on what we need to be free. For me, one of the most freeing and healing things I ever do is to take a few moments throughout the day to be grateful.

Why not choose to nurture a place of gratitude in our hearts? It has been said, "If you really want to be happy, no one can stop you."

Please excuse how glib this sounds. The harm people cause us can be devastating. The path to forgiveness can be extraordinarily difficult. It's just that forgiveness is so truly worth it. And the promise of the life, death, and resurrection of Jesus is that, in the big scheme of things, there is always more reason for joy than not.

One of my younger brothers is also a priest. (Our family is not very creative). He describes an interaction he saw during the Stations of the Cross, a devotional practice that remembers the steps of Jesus on his way to his unjust death on a cross. The eighth graders were presenting a form of "Living Stations," taking an element of each station and "freezing" into that position as the story was proclaimed. The first grade teacher was visibly moved by it all. It was at the thirteenth station—where Mary holds the dead body of her son—that her tears began to flow. The first grader right next to her noticed her teacher's tears. The little girl wrapped her hands around her teacher's arm and rested her head there for a moment. After a bit, she looked up and said, "Can I say something that might help?" "Of course," her teacher said. The little girl looked at her and said, "He didn't stay dead."

He didn't stay dead. Out of the mouths of babes, the deep truth for us. If Jesus did not remain in the grips of death, if the tomb could not—and would not—hold his one life, Jesus is showing us that it will not hold ours either. No matter how we have been harmed or mistreated, we don't have to stay dead either.

Bitter or better?

*Everything I've ever let go
has claw marks on it.*

DAVID FOSTER WALLACE

A friend of mine had been beaten by her dad as a child. Because the beatings would most often come at night, in her adult years, my friend found herself having trouble falling asleep. She knew well the words of Jesus that we are to forgive. As a person of goodness and integrity, she wanted to do that. But she wrestled with what forgiveness looked like in her circumstances, or whether or not she was even capable of it. Someone told her, "The fact that you desire to forgive him is enough for now. God will honor your willingness." Those words alone lifted the burden of what seemed like an impossible task and gave her the peace and freedom to trust that healing would eventually come.

How do we forgive? The first step is to have what my friend had in her heart. Her desire to forgive would itself make all the difference. No one can do it all by themselves; and no one has to. My friend's openness and willingness would be what allowed God to bring her the healing she needed.

There have been remarkable public examples of forgiveness. Journalist Terry Anderson was working in Beirut when he was kidnapped off a street and held hostage in Lebanon for more than six and a half years. He spent much of that time blindfolded and chained. When he publicly forgave his persecutors he said, "If I'm going to live as a Christian I have to forgive. It's a process. I'll be doing it for the rest of my life, I hope." When Nelson Mandela was released after being unjustly imprisoned for years and years, instead of seeking revenge or letting himself be filled with hatred, he sat down with his captors and began a process of healing and reconciliation. Pope John Paul II asked everyone to pray for the man who tried to kill him. Later, the pope visited his would-be assassin in prison to offer him forgiveness face to face. There is, of course, no more stunning example of forgiveness than the one that came from a brutalized Jesus hanging tortured on a cross and forgiving those who put him there.

How did they do that? What makes it possible? How does anyone ever forgive?

It has a lot to do with how we live our regular daily lives. The ways we have been mistreated leave us with the choice: will we become bitter or better? Spirituality has been described as that which allows us to move from one to the other.

There is always a "moment" between our feelings and what comes next. To help avoid a knee-jerk reaction that we later regret, we do well to name—in advance—how we would like to react, to be intentional about how we would like to be.

It is vital that we develop practices on a regular basis that nurture inner spaciousness, that help open "that moment" a bit more when it comes. Trying to live with integrity, working to keep perspective, practicing gratitude, connecting to that place inside us where we are both ourselves and more than ourselves, choosing to be kind, and understanding that our lives are not all about ourselves all help us to be ready to do the work of forgiveness when it is needed. It is almost always needed.

There is a Native American saying, articulated differently by different tribes: "There lives inside each person an eagle and a snake. We become the one we feed the most." The work of forgiveness feeds the best in us and frees the best in us.

It is lifelong work to become more loving human beings. Sometimes we take steps backward. Sometimes we take small steps forward. Sometimes the results are more dramatic.

So with forgiveness.

After the terrible years of apartheid in South Africa, the Truth and Reconciliation Commission set up by the Nelson Mandela government began its work of facilitating national healing. Remarkable stories of forgiveness and reconciliation emerged.

One such story describes a face-to-face encounter a woman had with the officer who had shot her eighteen-year-old son at point-blank range. This same man also admitted that he was the leader of the group that later came back and burned her husband alive, forcing her to watch as he died. She said that her husband's last words were "Forgive them."

When it was time for judgment, the Commission asked the woman what she wanted. She told them that she wanted three things. She first wanted to be brought to the place where her husband's body was burned so she could gather up the dust to give her husband a decent burial.

Then, since her husband and son were all the family she had, she wanted this officer to come to her impoverished township twice a month so she could be like a mother to him.

"Third," she said, "I would like this man to know that he is forgiven by God and that I forgive him too. Now I would like to embrace him so he can know forgiveness is real." As the woman was led across the courtroom, the officer fainted, overwhelmed. Someone began singing "Amazing Grace." Gradually everyone joined in.

The work of forgiveness engages that place inside of each of us where we are both ourselves and more than ourselves. There is that which we alone must do and that which we cannot do by ourselves. It is indeed an amazing grace.

Stumbling my way toward forgiveness...

*Everything can be taken
from a man [sic] but one thing:
the last of the human freedoms—
to choose one's attitude in any given
set of circumstances.*

VICTOR FRANKL

Once, a coworker and I sat down with a volunteer to tell him that—because of his inability to keep confidentiality—we would need to find a different role for him in the parish. My coworker and I practiced our conversation in advance and worked hard to be respectful. The man's response, however, was to hate me and try to make my life miserable. He seemed to put a lot of effort into his very public attempts to cause harm to me and to my reputation. After about a year of doing that, suddenly he stopped. Now he wanted to act like nothing had happened and become friends with me. Yikes!

My anger was justifiable. This man had done a lot of damage. Yet I did not want it to eat me up; I did not want to allow him to live "rent-free" in my head. But I just couldn't shake it. My coworker said to me, "You need to admit that you are powerless over your anger."

Though I have never worked a twelve-step program, I knew that an important element of that vital spiritual process was to admit that I could not do this by myself and needed to surrender it to God.

So, in order to give this man and my anger less power over me, I began a process of forgiveness. First, I typed up a document with all the ways he had hurt me so that I knew it was all recorded somewhere. From time to time I would go back to add more things or to tighten up what I had already written. The fact that I would replay the hurts again and again in my head seemed to be some sort of unconscious, self-protective mechanism. So it helped me to have it all safely stored somewhere else.

Then, I wrote a letter to God, naming my pain, asking for the help I needed, and surrendering all of it to God as best as I could. Then, I lit that letter on fire. As it burned, I prayed, doing my best to let go of all of it into the hands of the One who was all forgiveness.

That truly helped me tremendously…for exactly *seven minutes*! Then I remembered something else, and again felt the flash of anger. So I turned to God and said, "See, God. I can't do this by myself. You are going to have to help me. I again give this to you." That helped greatly for *eleven minutes* before I once more found myself angry.

So, I again surrendered it to God and asked for help, and did that again…and again…and again, until it no longer had any power over me at all. I don't remember how many months—or years—of doing that had passed, till one day I found myself thinking, "I would happily walk arm-in-arm into heaven with this guy." The man had no more power over me! If I were free on a Friday night, I would not choose to go get a beer with him, nor should I have to want to. But God had set me free.

My summary, then, of the three steps of forgiveness:

1. We make an act of the will and choose it.

2. We surrender it to God.

3. We do steps one and two again and again and again.

When Jesus tells Peter (Matthew 18:21, 22) we must forgive seventy times seven times, it might not be for that many different transgressions, but because we often feel anger again and again over the same wrongs!

Forgiveness is not a single act or decision. It is not a "one-and-done." Nor is the crucial journey of forgiveness a linear process. We start and stop, we stumble and we bumble, and we do the best we can in our own imperfect ways.

My friend who had been abused by her uncle put it this way: "People hurt us all the time. Sometimes it's really big stuff like screwing us out of jobs or stealing our spouses or killing our children. How do we move from bloodthirsty hatred to asking God to bless them and change me? The hardest prayer of all."

So, *how*, already?

You are braver than you believe,
stronger than you seem,
and smarter than you think.
WINNIE THE POOH

A parishioner was lamenting the damage he had caused to people he loved by the choices he had made. He said, "I wish my life were a notebook and I could just rip out those pages so that they never happened." Then he added, "It hurts deeply to look the people I love in the eyes and tell them I am sorry. I've got to try to make things right. It is just so brutally hard." He was doing the ninth step of a twelve-step program and found himself weeping with each person with whom he tried to make amends.

So did most of the people to whom he said he was sorry.

Just as we cannot "rip out" the pages of the pain we have caused to others, so we cannot just "rip out" the pain in our own hearts.

But there are steps we can take. There are things we can do. Because we are each so different, what helps will be different for each of us.

For me, I first need to be in touch with the mixture of emotions I feel. Becoming aware—without shaming ourselves—is always a key step toward growing in freedom.

Not everyone is like this, I guess, but it is much easier for me to let go of my angers if I first feel like I have said everything I could say. (Of course, it would help if the person would grovel, but, unfortunately, that usually is not going to happen). It is not always possible—or advisable—to speak directly to the person who hurt me. If I do think it would help, I work hard to prepare what I will say. My goal is not to shame that person but to bring myself honestly to them and to see if God might have something for them—or for me—to hear through that conversation.

Frequently, I talk to myself. I remind myself of those things I value, the wisdom of my faith tradition, and the insights that I have learned through so many good and faithful people down through the years. It is a foundational belief for me that—in the big scheme of things—there is always more reason for joy than not.

If the person is merely annoying, I sometimes ask, "God, you love that person, don't you?" So far, God's answer has always been "Yes."

When the hurt is more serious than mere annoyance, I usually remind myself how much I have been forgiven. Then I remind myself that no one can take away my dignity, and no one can take away my joy. I can give them away, but no one can take them from me.

Even though it helps me to remind myself of these things, it is often still so hard to let go. In the last chapter I mentioned a process and a ritual, both of which I find helpful.

A friend of mine has a different approach. She imagines that she is placing all of her hurts and burdens in a box that she ultimately places on the top shelf of her closet. She says, "Placing the box there is my way of relegating the hurts to a place where they are not in my way until I completely forget them. I am not denying or avoiding the pain. I am just intentionally choosing to pack the thoughts away as things I no longer want or need."

What helps you? Many find it helpful to talk confidentially to a trusted friend, spiritual guide, or counselor. For many who love someone who struggles with addiction, twelve-step groups have proven an invaluable resource for the essential spiritual work of healthy detachment. Others have developed spiritual practices that help them draw on the power that is both in them and also more than them.

The process of "transitioning to something more positive" is ongoing and usually messy. As essential as the work of forgiveness is, it is also difficult.

When I get a bit discouraged about feeling beaten up along the way, I sometimes think of one of my heroes, Fr. Gregory Boyle, who works to help young folks become free of a life of gang violence in the L.A. region. Someone asked him how he handles his discouragements and if he had any wisdom for us in that regard. He said simply: "We have to love being loving."

Forgiveness is one of those things that Jesus asks that could seem to be almost impossible to do. But I've seen it with my own eyes and known it in my own heart.

Some years ago, the parish where I was blessed to serve experienced the tragic death of a young man named Shawn. Shawn was a graduate of our parish grade school, a delightful young man, outgoing, generous, well-liked, and much-loved.

Shawn died a heartbreaking death at age twenty-three in a senseless car wreck. The driver, whose mistake did much to cause the accident, was hospitalized but lived. Before the funeral started, I was talking to Shawn's dad, Mike, near the front of church. Mike is a huge man. He is a quiet person who loves the outdoors, and he is so big that when I hug him, I disappear in his arms.

As Mike and I were talking, the young man who had been driving the car arrived. He had gotten a release from the hospital and was brought to church in an ambulance. As he came through the doors of church in a wheelchair, Mike saw him. Mike said, "Excuse me, Father," and walked toward this young man. As Mike approached his wheelchair, he towered over it. I did not know what was going to happen and for a moment held my breath. What did happen was that Mike got down on his knees in front of this young man, held out his arms, and hugged him. They held on to each other and both cried in each other's arms.

I say it again: Forgiveness is one of those things that Jesus asks that could seem to be almost impossible to do. But I've seen it with my own eyes and known it in my own heart.

The family wound...

*I have always thought the term
"Dysfunctional family" is redundant.*
IRA BYOCK

Once I visited a buddy of mine while his two children played in the other room. The younger one started to get on his big sister's nerves, and we overheard her—in an attempt to get her younger brother to behave—say to him: "If you don't stop that, Daddy isn't going to love you anymore." My friend knew it was one of "those moments," so he went into the room (while I peeked through the crack between the door and the wall). He put one child on each leg and said to them: "It is very important to me that you understand this. Your daddy loves you always. When you behave well, I love you with a happy heart. When you misbehave, I love you with a sad heart. But I will always love you."

Those children are fortunate to have such a father. They will be able—perhaps more than many—to understand the incredible love of God and the forgiveness that is available to them.

Not every child is nearly as fortunate.

From our parents we each receive two significant things: our greatest blessings and our deepest wounds. We are each blessed by our parents; we are each wounded by them.

It is true that the best qualities of our moms and dads capture a little bit of the incredible goodness in the heart of God. God embodies those things at their purest and deepest. But God is so much more. And the ways our parents wounded us? God is not like those in any way.

If we live with great dysfunction in our family, when we are the one who gets healthy, the family system typically turns on us. Suddenly *we* become the "bad one." And yes, the ones we love can hurt us the most.

We find ways to cope as a child. Thank goodness. Those who were sexually abused often learn to dissociate; those who feared love might go away often become perfectionists or pleasers; those raised in unpredictable situations often reject their own inner guidance and latch on to some outer system for security. Sadly, the same coping skills that helped us get through when we were children become a challenge to our growth in freedom as we get older.

But we've got to do the work. As Franciscan priest Richard Rohr says, what we do not transform we will transmit.

It inspires me to watch people who do the difficult painful work of becoming more free so as to break the circle of violence. We do not have to pass on to others those same wounds or hurts we received growing up.

Of course, there are all different types of challenges. Whether it is being related to someone who is alcoholic or drug-dependent, dreading the holidays because of the tension, or dealing with the effects of depression, autism, illness, or grief, being a part of a family is just so difficult.

Whether we are struggling with Dad's new wife, or Mom's new husband, and how weird that is; or living with the results of a divorce that we didn't want; or trying to care for a parent who does not agree they have dementia, family is messy.

Wonderfully, our amazing God chose to make a home in human mess. The One who created the universe and all that is in it was humbly born into the mess of a human family as an infant in Bethlehem.

It was a birth unlike what's typically depicted in Christmas cards. Most are simply much too pretty. Jesus was not born into a Christmas-card world. Jesus was born into mess: a physical, smelly mess; the family mess of a poor, betrothed mother; the political mess of a time of great turmoil and strife. The family would soon be on the run for their lives.

We do not grow up in "Christmas-card worlds" either. Some of our family dynamics are simply annoying. Some of the changes we face are to be expected, while some come as shocking and horrific tragedy. Some of our family life is scary. Some of it is sad, some of it is fun, and most of it is messy. But that is exactly the type of place Jesus chose to call "home." In the mixture of all of that, God is to be found.

One of the most important sentences I ever heard is only six words long. It comes in response to the question, "How does God come to you?" The answer? God comes disguised as your life.

Yes, God comes disguised as our lives. There is no other way God comes. We have no other life. In the humor, God is there laughing with us. In the beauty, God is there to delight with us. In the challenge, God is there to inspire us. In the heartache and the wounds, God is there to hold us.

Inner bumper stickers

The mind is its own place,
and in itself can make a Heaven of Hell,
a Hell of Heaven. **JOHN MILTON**

T hough they are not nearly as popular as they once were, bumper stickers still show up on some cars. Recently I saw one that made me laugh. It offered its encouragement through a somewhat pessimistic view of human nature:

> Don't worry about what people think:
> They don't do it very often.

Whether or not we personally put bumper stickers on our cars, we each carry around *inner* bumper stickers: the ways we talk to ourselves in the course of a day. These—often unspoken—internal messages affect what we decide to do or not do. They greatly affect how we think and what we feel. Though they can have great power in our lives, often we are only somewhat aware of them, if at all.

Most commonly, we learn them as children.

My dad was a good man, and I loved him. Yet, growing up, what I most dreaded was the look my dad gave me when he was disappointed in me. It would have been better for me if he had just gotten crabby. Instead, Dad would sometimes slowly shake his head, look right at me, and give me *the look* (the same look, I would imagine, that he got from his dad). The look felt to me that he was trying to tell me that he was disgusted with me. It led to one of my key inner bumper stickers: "I'm not good enough."

That unspoken mantra caused a lot of pain in my life—and shows up even now sometimes.

Maybe you know that inner bumper sticker or one of its cousins: "I am stupid"; "I don't fit in"; "No one wants me or loves me." For many, the inner bumper stickers are fear-based: "The world is a scary place, and I should be afraid." Or "People will take advantage of me: Don't trust anyone." Some develop inner bumper stickers for which the word "should" is pivotal. "I should be perfect." "You should appreciate me at all times." "They should change."

The possibilities are almost endless. Whatever the inner bumper stickers, we've all got them. They not only affect us; they also deeply affect our relationships with others.

An important step toward flourishing as persons is to become aware of those things we tell ourselves—consciously or unconsciously—about ourselves and

this world. There is no need for shame, just for awareness. In the spiritual world, awareness is everything! It
helps if we can get someone to walk an inner journey
with us to help us name these things, to understand
where they come from, and to begin to replace those
inner, self-defeating messages with others that give life.

When I do that work and name healthier inner
bumper stickers for myself, I then need to practice
them. Whether I tape them to my mirror or set them
as a reminder in my phone, I do simple things to help
me more quickly turn to those thoughts rather than the
ones that are harmful.

Stress elevates the level of negative self-talk. When I
get overwhelmed by the demands of a seemingly impossible workload, I've learned to tell myself: "God is alive
in this world and it does not all depend on me." It is a
grace for me to remember moments when God showed
me how true that was.

When I am too far behind and life seems to be going
past too quickly, I slow myself down by remembering:
"There is only *now*. All the love in the universe is with
me here and now."

Drawing on that inner bumper sticker often helps
ease my breathing and calm my stomach.

Once, when I began a new assignment in a parish
that was struggling, I was overwhelmed. But my mantra
became: "Savor the blessings; trust the chaos." It was
the right inner bumper sticker for me. It still comes in
handy now.

These days, when people ask me how I am doing, I usually answer them: "My problems are small. My blessings are huge." It is true. And when I say that out loud, I am reminded of just how true it is.

What are your inner bumper stickers? Do they give you life? It is particularly important to be able to name them for those times we are wronged, betrayed, or taken advantage of. Otherwise, the negative internal messages will have a power over us with consequences we don't want.

In response to our hurts, for some, the unnamed mantra becomes "They must pay for that." For others, the default thought is "I am no good: it must be my fault." Some slip into "Don't trust anyone." Or it might be "That doesn't bother me," even when it does.

I don't know what your bumper stickers are, but you and I both have them. And I believe they matter. Are you willing to do the work to name them and to replace some with healthier ones? As has been said, what we don't deal with will deal with us.

Who are you?

Define yourself radically as one beloved by God. This is the true self. Every other identity is illusion.

BRENNAN MANNING

Researchers at Harvard University did a study that was reported in the July 3, 2014, issue of the journal *Science*. They put people in a room with the option of either sitting in silence for fifteen minutes or choosing to interrupt their silence by inflicting a physical shock to their system.

The results were stunning (so to speak). Their study showed that many people would rather experience a significant physical shock than to endure fifteen minutes of uninterrupted silence. Two-thirds of the men and one-fourth of the women found sitting in silence so unbearable that they chose to administer an electric shock to themselves instead.

We do many things to keep ourselves distracted from silence, perhaps not always intentionally, but with the effect of doing so. You know the ways.

One of the reasons for this, I suggest, is that we don't want to experience the emptiness we fear is at the heart of ourselves or to be reminded of the painful wounds we carry. We have not become friends with the depths of who we are. We fear the inner journey, because often we first have to sink through a yuckier level of memories and feelings to get to that place where we can sit peacefully in the silence of God's goodness. *Heavenly Place!*

The wounds are there. We have all levels of hurt, coming from many sources: Be it parents who pushed us too hard; sexual abuse by family members or others; the struggles with eating that grew from our yearning to know we fit in; the fear that others would not welcome our sexual orientation (maybe we're not sure we welcome it ourselves); the pain of a failed marriage and the hopes that died along with it; the ways we have been mistreated; perhaps some pattern of addiction; sin; shame. Whatever it is that we might find in there: we fear it.

Yet we are *all* wounded. And unfortunately, most of us have not learned well the truth that it is okay to be wounded. Well, it is.

A woman I know described what she called "the lowest part" of her life. She was going through an awful divorce and was afraid to go home at night because of the physical and verbal abuse that awaited her. One day she selected the place where she would drive off the road to end her life. Thankfully, before she did that, she first thought to call her best friend, who told her, "It's okay not to be okay." She said, "Those words saved my life."

It *is* okay not to be okay. When we venture inward, we often first meet those places in us where we don't feel peaceful and whole but rather feel frightened or confused, trapped or resentful, lonely or heartsick. It's enough to make many, if not most, people avoid the journey inside altogether. But we do not need to be afraid to embrace some silence. It is the path to fullness of life!

We would do well, then, to perhaps take more walks, get some quiet time in church, jot some thoughts in an occasional journal, or let someone we trust walk inside our life story with us. However we do it, it is an important journey.

The good news is that there is no hurt that could surface within us that we can't deal with. There is no pain or suffering that is beyond God's healing grace. There are good people who are smart and skilled who can help us. We do not need to fear what lies within. Nothing we will find diminishes our goodness. We are no less important or lovable to God because we are broken.

Nor do we need to fix ourselves or even completely understand ourselves. We just name what we find and bring it to God, who cares more deeply than we could understand or imagine. God delights in our honesty. One of my priest friends said it this way: "These days when I pray, I see myself as the infant who does not yet know how to talk, so who simply holds up something for others to see. That's what I do: I just hold myself and my stuff before God for God to see."

This difficult, never-ending journey is the single most important one we could ever make. For underneath what people see on the outside, below all that we feel and think, is no less than a child of God: intact and good, wanted and loved, unique and important, seen and safe, and deeply united with the God who created us and whose love will never end.

A friend of mine once described something he witnessed while volunteering at the Special Olympics. A group of young men with Down's Syndrome was running around the track in their big race when one of the racers near the back slipped and fell, scraping his knee as he did so and crying out in pain. The runner who was leading the race heard him cry, stopped, and turned around. When he saw the young man down on the track, he started to walk back toward him, and the other runners also stopped. When he got to the young man who had fallen, he said, "It's okay," bent over, and helped him to his feet. Then, he put his arm around his shoulder and started walking with him toward the finish line. Soon the other runners joined them, locked arms over each other's shoulders, and walked the final part of the race together. With the crowd on its feet enthusiastically cheering them on, the group of runners together walked across the finish line arm in arm. They were all winners.

So it is with all of us. Together we walk arm in arm in our weakness toward the finish line: wounded, imperfect, beloved children of God.

Recalculating

Wisdom doesn't necessarily come with age.
Sometimes age just shows up all by itself.
TOM WILSON

Ask anyone who knows me well and they will tell you that I am horrible with directions. That's because I am. Unfortunately, I am also no good at reading maps. So I will never forget how amazed I was many years ago when my good friend Jerry described to me this new invention called the GPS. (Yes, I lived before those were invented). It seemed too good to be true. Not only would this device tell me which way to turn; it would tell me how much distance there was until I needed to make that turn!

My travel anxiety decreased as greatly as my travel efficiency increased. Yet, sometimes, even with my GPS, I'd still manage to miss a turn or find myself on a detour of one kind or another. (One would think I would have learned to stop questioning this seemingly magical device.)

Given my tendency to move toward shame when I mess up, one of the things I particularly love about my GPS is that it never tries to make me feel bad. Mercifully, whenever I find myself on the wrong road, my GPS does not scold me. Instead, it offers one wonderful word. You might have heard this word. It is "recalculating." When I miss an exit, it does not say, "Turn around, you moron." Or, "Pay attention, for crying out loud." It simply says, "Recalculating."

If either the road I am on or the direction I am heading is not the best way to get me where I want to go, my GPS tells me where I next need to turn, and in which direction, to get me to where I was hoping to go.

So it is with God's call.

Out of immeasurable love, God wants to lead us on paths that give life. Jesus never pretends it is an easy journey. But because he so greatly wants us to know life—now, and at the hour of our death—Jesus invites us to follow him on the way. The early followers of Jesus were actually called "people of the way," for his way truly is the way to life. Jesus walked that painful, beautiful journey before us, and there has never been a person more alive and free than he was.

As did his early followers, you and I often need a certain amount of recalculating along the way to get to where we say we want to go. It's fair to say, I think, that most people want meaningful, joy-filled lives. There is a longing in each of us for true connection, authentic happiness, vibrant love, and deep peace.

The question? Is the path we are on leading us there? On the journey of life, are we taking the right steps to get us where we are meant to be, where we want to be?

Or not?

We might say that we don't want to be crabby, angry people who walk through our lives making others miserable. Yet, unless we are self-aware, that might be exactly the direction we are heading.

How many of us carry unnecessary burdens of anger and bitterness, unaware that doing so drags us down and keeps us from getting where we want to go? Again the question: on the journey of life, are we on the paths that will get us to where we want to be?

If we find we have strayed off the path—in big ways or small—God never shames us. No, God is much too delighted by the goodness in the human heart to try to make us feel bad. Nor does our own self-loathing move us any further down the road toward a beautiful life. If we truly want to be people who are kind, grateful, and joyful, God simply and urgently asks, "Are you moving in the right direction?"

No, God's call does not come with shame. Instead, it carries a crucial invitation to recalculate. God lovingly says, "This is the direction toward a deeper, more beautiful life. Join me. For not only did I go that way before you, I am with you now and each step of the way."

Perfectionism

Ring the bells that still can ring
Forget your perfect offering
There is a crack in everything
That's how the light gets in.
LEONARD COHEN

When I was a child (in the early 1800s, I think), I read the book *The Little Engine That Could*. It's the story of a train full of food and toys for children on the other side of a very high mountain. The train needs an engine to pull it, and an unlikely tiny blue engine wants to try. Though it is a huge task, the little engine repeats again and again, "I think I can, I think I can. I think I can, I think I can." Spoiler alert: The little engine can; it makes it! The moral of the story seems to be: If you believe in yourself, you will achieve great things!

There is some value in such thinking. It is good to believe that we are people who can make a difference in this world. But there is also something quite dangerous about thinking that if we *believe* we can do something, then we *will* succeed. That concept often turns into, "I *must* succeed; I *must* succeed." And we can grow up with the notion that failure is unacceptable. While a positive attitude is helpful, there are situations where we can say, "I think I can, I think I can," and try with all our might, but still cannot. Maybe the train is too heavy, the mountain too high, or our engine too small.

Of course, we need to give truly important things our effort. Yet failure is the norm. It is unfair to leave kids unprepared for those times they don't succeed.

We all fail sometimes.

Once, when Jesus sent his followers out to preach the good news, he added an interesting piece of coaching. He warned them that sometimes they would experience rejection and failure. When that happens, Jesus told them, they were to then *shake the dust from their feet* and move on. Jesus does not want us to let our failures eat us up. When we fail, we are to acknowledge our loss and keep going. Jesus wants us and all his followers to be able to "shake it off."

For many of us, the work of shaking it off is difficult. Yet it is it truly important.

For the reality is that failure happens! Business plans don't always work out. Not every marriage is made in heaven. Not every surgery is successful. Not every new product is a winner. Most students in college don't make honors. Friendships are full of missteps, mistakes, and misstatements. Maybe we should not be so surprised when these things happen.

We human beings are finite and fallible. Perhaps Jesus is saying, in so many words, "Get over it!" Some things that are broken cannot be fixed. Some relationships aren't going to take off. Most kids in sports programs get cut way before ever getting to the college or professional level. Parents can do all the right things, and yet their child may still suffer, may still go astray. And it is okay. You and I are still beloved of God.

We can get so stuck in our remorse that we miss the life that we have. We can spend so much inner energy on self-recrimination that we miss the opportunities to do good right in front of us.

Instead of berating ourselves for our human frailty, I believe that God would have us learn to acknowledge it, admit our failures, trust the promise of forgiveness, and move on. You and I are more than the sum of our failures and mistakes. May God help us shake the dust of regret from those feet of ours!

If I had had kids, perhaps I would have read them *The Little Engine That Could*. If so, I hope I would have also added my own stories about the little engines that couldn't. And, instead of always saying, "I think I can, I think I can," I'd make sure my children knew that it would be okay if sometimes they said, "I *don't* think I can."

Forgiving yourself...

The more you know yourself,
the more you forgive yourself.
CONFUCIUS

There is a story that when Thomas Edison was working on improving his first lightbulb, he handed a finished bulb to a young helper who nervously carried it upstairs. Near the top of the steps the boy dropped the precious bulb and it shattered. After a moment of horrified silence, the whole team set back to work. With many hours of hard work, they finished another bulb. When it was ready to be taken upstairs again, Edison looked around, found the same boy, and handed the bulb to him to do the job. Edison purposefully gave the kid another chance in order to show him that he still believed in him.

Can you do that for yourself?

Trying to accept forgiveness can be as hard as offering it. For many, it is truly difficult to give ourselves a new beginning.

It's especially difficult to offer ourselves that compassion when there is someone who refuses to forgive us or who continues to throw our mistakes in our faces.

Often enough, we don't even need another person to try to make us feel bad again. We do it ourselves. Our shame just grabs us.

Growing up, when I messed up, my temptation was always to feel shame. In other words, instead of healthily critiquing my mistakes, I let any bad behavior on my part—even if unintentional—tell me that *I* must be bad. Unfortunately, I could not see in me what God saw— that I don't have to be perfect to be lovable.

There are many spiritual writers who would tell us that—on some levels—the opposite is true. In the spiritual realm we actually grow much more by doing it wrong than by doing it right. When we sin or fail, we can no longer live under the delusion that we are "earning" love. We can no longer sustain the notion that we are better than "those people." We remember again that we are all much more alike than different.

As has been said, God does not love us because we are good, but we are good because God loves us. We are tempted to make worthiness something that is ours to achieve. But we can't earn God's love. More important, we don't have to!

When Peter said to Jesus, "Depart from me, Lord, for I am a sinful man," Jesus did *not* depart from him. Or, as I sometimes hear myself say to people who are filled with shame: "You don't have enough power to make God stop loving you!"

Some twenty or thirty years ago I was hearing grade-school confessions when a young girl, a scared kind of kid, maybe fourth or fifth grade, told me her sins. As I sometimes do, I asked her two questions. First, I asked: "Are you sorry for that?" She said, "Yes." Then I asked, "Why are you sorry?" She got this frightened, far-away look in her eyes and said in her quiet, scared voice, "I want God to love me again." I could have cried.

As if God would ever stop loving her.

Sometimes I think that parents have a unique insight into the heart of God. If you are a parent or grandparent of a young one, you might have experienced a child's temper tantrum. As exasperating as that is, you didn't stop loving that child, did you? Some parents tell me that—no matter how frustrating their interactions with their child have been on any given day—watching their child sleeping reminds them again of how much they love that child. If you are a mom or dad, I would argue that the love that wells up in your heart at moments like that is not only what God is like; it actually *is* God in you.

And if you can still love the child who drove you nuts that day, if you still long for the child who has gone astray, will not God do the same with you?

That long journey from head to heart

The greatest act of faith some days is to simply get up and face another day.

AMY GATLIFF

There is an old story that, after Jesus was raised from the dead and had ascended into heaven, there was to be a big party to celebrate. The heavenly banquet table was ready, but Jesus was nowhere to be found. So the disciples sent Peter to go looking for Jesus. After a while Peter came back and they asked him where Jesus was. Peter said, "He's at the gates of heaven. Jesus said he is waiting for Judas."

There is something in the heart of Jesus that will always wait for us. Jesus knows that we are more than our sin, more than our biggest failure.

You and I? We might know that intellectually, but that news doesn't always travel easily from our head down to our gut. How do we move forward when guilt and shame haunt us?

50

When we have hurt someone, there is that which we need to do. When we have caused harm to ourselves, to another, or to this world, we have a responsibility to deal with that. If possible, we first find a way to say we are sorry to the right people. When we do so, we need to take great care, because *how* we say we are sorry is deeply important. Second, we need to make amends wherever possible. Usually, we can never completely undo the damage we've done, but we must do what we can.

When we've done that, and we've also told God we're sorry, for many of us it is now time for the work of self-forgiveness, for moving forward instead of backward. Even though it might be hard for us to completely trust this, we do well to first remind ourselves that God has forgiven us, because, well, that's just what God does.

Then, when remorse grabs at our gut again, instead of going backward into shame, we use that moment to make a conscious decision to do something loving. In thanksgiving for the mercy we have received from God, perhaps we are kind to the person nearby, whisper a prayer for someone who is hurting, or reach out in an act of service as needed right then.

Forgiving ourselves, like forgiving others, is an intentional process. Each time we start to feel bad again, we remind ourselves that we have been forgiven and choose to love again in that moment. The process of letting go of our shame, accepting forgiveness, and forgiving ourselves does not happen all at once, and perhaps it is never completely finished. But if we keep choosing to be loving when we again feel ashamed, over time, our sin and failure can themselves become key elements of our transformation into becoming more loving human beings for the world!

A friend of mine is trying to learn to have compassion for herself. She said: "Knowing that God forgives me is not enough. But it is not hard for me to have compassion for others who are hurting. So I think of someone who is really struggling or knows great heartache and feel my compassion for them. Then I go to that part of me where I feel inadequate, flawed, or broken and try to duplicate that same feeling for myself. It's hard work. But I know I need to do it."

I'm not sure what helps *you* on the path toward forgiving yourself, but it is truly important that you try. There is a guided prayer experience later in the book that you might find of some benefit.

Whatever helps, however you do it, this work, though difficult for many, helps free us for what God has called us to do in the time that is ours in this world.

Once there was a young monk who went to his superior, the abbot, to tell him that Jesus was appearing to him, face to face, during his prayer time. The abbot knew that the young monk was a good man, but he had his doubts about this. After listening, the abbot said: "I know you're a sincere young man, but this is just so unusual." He paused and said, "I tell you what: If Jesus appears to you again, ask him what sins I confessed in the Sacrament of Reconciliation the week before. And if it really is Jesus, then he should know." The young monk agreed, and they met a week later. The abbot asked him: "Did Jesus appear to you again this week?" "Yes." "And you asked him what sins I confessed this past weekend in the Sacrament of Reconciliation?" "I did." "And what did Jesus say?" The young monk looked directly at the abbot and said: "Jesus told me that I was to look you right in the eyes and tell you that his answer is: 'I forgot.'"

You or I might be someone who can't seem to forget our mistakes. But God is not as interested in our past mistakes and failures as we are. Instead, God looks us in the eyes and says, "I love you—right now. Let's go. Let's go love this world."

Must I forgive God?

*We must let go of God
in order to find God.*

ECKHART

A woman I know was cleaning her bathroom and talking to God about the abuse she had experienced as a child. Not only had her dad sexually abused her, but her dad had also invited his brother to participate. She said, "I would always ask God: 'Why did you let that happen, God? Why, God, why? Why didn't you stop it?'" She said, "One day, as I was cleaning the bathroom and scrubbing the side of the toilet, I knew the answer. It was as if, without words, God said to me: 'They were free. If I forced them to do anything, I would be just like them.'" And this woman cried with relief because she knew—and she *knew* that she knew— that God was not like her dad or her uncle. Going forth, and forever, she knew that what happened to her was not God's fault.

The sufferings of this world are *not* God's idea. Unfortunately, many of the clichés we use at funeral homes, hospital beds, or other times of suffering suggest differently.

You've heard them. Perhaps you've said them. I sure hope you don't believe what they seem to suggest: that God kills people or sends suffering. Statements like "God never gives you more than you can handle" or "God never closes a door without opening a window" seem to suggest that *God* sends us suffering for some higher purpose. Even the ubiquitous phrase "Everything happens for a reason" is greatly problematic. Yes, God can bring something good from the things life throws at us. Who has not experienced some blessing that was born of struggle? But that does not mean that God was the one who caused the bad thing to happen.

Two things are true simultaneously: God does *not* send us suffering or death, and it is *okay* to be angry at God! God can handle our anger. The God I know yearns for our honesty in prayer. If we can't bring ourselves to God as we are—with all our angers, hurts, and confusions—what kind of God would that be? It is better to have it out with God than to just slip away from the relationship.

Even if we don't believe God sends us suffering, for many there is an unformulated sense that God must be aloof from our pain and anguish. If God is not causing it, God must not care. God must be detached or unaware. Again I ask, what kind of God would that be? Not one with whom I would be interested in a relationship.

Any inclinations to imagine God as aloof from our

pain and suffering were forever given lie to by the cru-
cifixion, an image of which hangs in every Catholic
institution and most Catholic homes. Sadly, it is an
image we usually quite glibly pass by, unaware.

The image of this reviled and bloodied victim dying
a tortuous death on a cross stands forever for us as the
most powerful statement of the love of God: the God
who has embraced our human suffering, the God who—
in Jesus—suffers *with* us!

There is a stunning story in the Gospel of John about
what happened when one of Jesus' friends died. When
Jesus arrives at the tomb that held the lifeless body of his
friend Lazarus, Jesus first does this amazing thing: He
weeps. Yes, Jesus weeps. God, in Jesus, knows what it is
like to hurt, to know loss, to be hardly able to breathe at
the sadness of death and at the pain of the others whose
hearts have also been broken.

Then, as Jesus stands before Lazarus' tomb, perhaps
his face still wet from tears, he does the second most
amazing thing: He calls Lazarus forth into life again.
And Lazarus comes forth from the tomb. Jesus calls life
from death.

Those two things, I believe, are what Jesus does with
us. He weeps with us. He calls forth life from our heartaches and losses.

No, God does not *cause* suffering or death. Instead,
God first takes on our every suffering, then stands, so to
speak, before the tombs of our lives and calls us forth.
And in that call comes the power to bring life and mean-

ing from what is heartache and loss.

Must I forgive God? No. Please just make sure that the God against whom you hold a grudge is really who God is.

How do I know if I've truly forgiven someone?

It is easier to forgive an enemy than to forgive a friend.

WILLIAM BLAKE

The message on my voicemail ended with the question: "So, how do I know if I've truly forgiven her, Fr. Joe?" Some fourteen months earlier this caller had described to me his heartache at his wife's infidelity, at the money she'd siphoned away unbeknownst to him, and at the fact that she one day decided to simply walk out, leaving behind a lot of heartache and loss.

When I first met him I could tell he was a good guy, trying to do what is right and to be whom he is called to be. He has done his best to help heal his hurting family, to not become bitter, and to take the high road when talking with her or about her. But the question haunted him: "How do I know if I've truly forgiven her?"

My honest answer would be, "I don't know, and I don't think that question really matters that much."

That was not, of course, the first thing I said. Instead, I listened and loved the man as best I could. At one point I asked him, "Why do you think it's important to you to know if you've 'truly forgiven her'?" He said, "Father, I want to do this right. I just don't want God to be disappointed in me."

What do you think: Is God disappointed in him? From everything I can see, this man is doing the work that God wants him to do. It is understandable that he still has occasional flashes of hurt and anger. At the same time, he is working to be a loving human being for his family and for this world. Do you think God would ask more?

Unfortunately, as mentioned elsewhere in this book, too many of us are easily caught up in a certain amount of perfectionism. This temptation shows up even around our efforts to forgive. What kind of God would expect perfection from us imperfect creatures? Our efforts to try to "do it just right" can get in the way of the healing that needs to happen.

If we take time to reflect, we can usually tell when our angers have less power over us. We can see signs that we are becoming more free of the pain, less caught up in our bitterness, less hungry for revenge.

It is not unusual that—seemingly out of the blue—we are suddenly again angry at something that we thought we had mostly worked through. So what? There it is. We name it, but don't panic. If we start to spiral down again into rage or resentment, then it is time to become more intentional about the work of surrendering it all to a higher power and to do those things that help us let go, that help us become more alive.

Who knows if we ever completely let go of our hurts?

More important, if we are not being eaten up by the pain, if we are functioning—imperfectly, of course—as mostly good, loving human beings, are we not on the right track?

If we are trying to forgive, and are doing the hard work of being a loving person for the world: Is that not enough? If we asked God, I believe that God's answer would be, "Yes. Yes, it is."

How much depends on *you*?

*When you come to the edge of all the
light you know and are about to step off
into the darkness of the unknown, faith is
knowing one of two things will happen:
There will be something solid to
stand on or you will be taught to fly.*

PATRICK OVERTON

For sixteen years I had been blessed to serve as
pastor at a parish that had become my home. My
years there held for me countless blessings, tons
of work, plenty of heartache, and the gift of deep con-
nections with a people I came to love. When my time
there was at an end, people were truly gracious in their
goodbye. When I left, I did so grateful for their love, and
grateful that they would be in the hands of a priest I
knew was a good man.

Yet, it was really tough to go. But that day quickly
came, and I turned in my keys and drove away. When
I got to the bridge over the river that divides the two
counties, I suddenly started sobbing so hard I was

afraid I would crash. There was no place to pull over on the bridge, so I just kind of aimed my car straight ahead and tried to drive.

When I arrived at my new parish, of course, I found new challenges, and some of what I initially met left me a bit frightened.

Soon I was at my first Sunday Mass at my new parish. My gut held a mixture of things: I was nervous, hopeful, a bit overwhelmed, and the sadness of goodbye still weighed heavily on me. When we got to the front singing the opening song, I felt something tug on my songbook. The little fifth-grade server was pulling down my hymnal a bit so that she could also sing along. It was such a simple thing, but with her earnestness I found tears at the edges of my eyes. In that simple moment it was as if God said to me, "I am here."

I don't know how the challenges and letting-gos will find you. But they will. Nor do I know how God will say to you, "I am here," but I believe God will.

The work of forgiveness, like all our efforts to grow into the full human beings we were meant to be, is a lot of work. It requires our openness and willingness to do what is required. But it does not all depend on us.

Jesus has promised to be with us to empower us with what we need no matter what we face. There is nowhere we could ever go that God is not already there. And sometimes when we aren't looking for it—in us or around us—what we need just shows up. With or without words, God will say, "I am here."

We are wise when we realize that we cannot do it all by ourselves. We are also wise when we realize we do not need to.

Some years ago, at a stressful time in my life, I had a bit of time away to try to work and pray. There were too many deadlines, too many things not going well, and my stress level was really, really high. I had the gift of seventy-two hours at a beautiful retreat center—and the challenge of getting about 720 hours' worth of work done. It was too much. I just couldn't find peace.

A single line from something I was reading came as great grace in the midst of the stress. The writer pointed out that our Scriptures do not say that Jesus "raised himself" from the dead. They say that Jesus "was raised" from the dead. Jesus did not raise himself!

It was almost as if a physical pressure was taken off my shoulders. Jesus didn't raise himself from the dead; I don't have to raise myself either. It does not all depend on me.

No matter how much work I do on myself, there are always times when my life's wounds again grab my gut, when the old insecurities again attempt to wrestle my thoughts to the ground. My temptation has always been to think, "Oh, no. I'm back at the very beginning again." What I have come to understand is that, as I grow in freedom, I run into the effects of my wounds less often, but I will still run into them. In times of crises the spiral tightens and my issues are more in my face again. But that does not mean I am back at the beginning.

When Jesus was raised from the dead, he still bore the marks of the wounds in his body. They just had no more power over him. That is ultimately the place God wants to take me with my own wounds.

And always there is a power in me that is a part of me and more than me. There is a loving God at the heart of the universe and in every single moment. Jesus never promised we won't be mistreated, suffer, or even be killed. He never says that every*thing* will be okay. Jesus promises to be in it with us to raise us up. I draw on that power; I choose to trust that power. I do what I can, but I know that it is not *me* who does the raising.

What helps you?

Why do we only rest in peace?
Why don't we live in peace too?

I t was the second graders' turn to do the readings at our all-school Mass. One of our young ones who was scheduled to read at that Mass was sick the day before and missed the practice. When she arrived at school the next day her teacher asked her if she would be okay to do the reading that morning. She said, "Oh, yes, I practiced at home." Her teacher said, "No, I mean, do you *feel* good enough to do it?" The little second grader said, "Oh, I'm fine. It was just *morning* sickness."

Fortunately, life is funny sometimes. Laughter is one of the things that helps me be okay in a sometimes-painful world. What helps you?

When flight attendants tell us that "oxygen masks will drop from the ceiling should we lose compression" (talk about faith), they ask us to put our own masks on first if we are traveling with someone who needs assistance. The first time I heard that recommendation, I wasn't sure I agreed. That is, until a mom pointed out that—if a child resisted putting his or her mask on and I passed out while trying to help—we would likely both die.

In times of intense crisis or challenge, the oxygen mask we need to keep on looks like four things. The first three are physical: Sleep, exercise, and nutrition. The fourth is to daily do something that nurtures our souls, that helps our spirits breathe. Of course, it is important to keep these as part of our living on a regular basis as well.

At the most stressful times, it can help to keep it simple. Someone made that clear to me on the night my dad died. My dad, just about the age I am now, had suffered a brain aneurysm while out buying a Christmas tree with my mom. He died that night without ever regaining consciousness. Many well-intentioned people—in an attempt to be helpful—said useless things. There was one thing, however, that someone said that was actually helpful. Someone said to me: "Keep breathing." Sometimes, that was about all I felt I could do. In the midst of our worst times, perhaps one of the things we can do is remind ourselves to "keep breathing."

When we grapple with our reactions to the harm that others have caused us, denial doesn't help. Violent or addictive behaviors only make things worse. Instead, we need to keep an oxygen mask on.

And if you ever find yourself in a dark place and start to think about how to end your life, please, please call someone you trust. Suicide is an awful decision: a permanent solution to a temporary problem. It leaves too many people angry and broken. No, you don't have to deal with your struggles alone. There is help. There is. And keep breathing.

Whatever the traumas we live through, it is important that we are intentional about including in our lives those things that help keep us keep healthy and alive. So what does help you? It is good to name those things for ourselves.

For me, quiet time in nature is truly healing. Others take extra time to read. What a gift it can be to have the support of a faith community who can believe for us when it is hard for us to do so, who can pray for us when it is hard for us to pray.

Often a trusted counselor is crucial. As we go through life, we learn who the people are to whom we can turn. We learn to not angrily dwell on those who won't be there for us. Instead, we just go to those we know will be.

And, if possible, it can help to keep our eyes open for things that make us laugh. It has been well said: "The young man who has not wept is a savage, and the older man who will not laugh is a fool."

Recently we planned music for our school Masses for the upcoming year. We wanted to compile a list of all the songs we had used the previous year. Rather than typing each of them, while one person scrolled through the pages of our planning sheets on her computer, I dictated them into my phone. Siri changed one word when transcribing the title of the lovely song "The Lord is Kind and Merciful." The word *and* became *of*. It made me laugh out loud when I read the new title: "The Lord is Kind of Merciful."

Fortunately, the Lord is much more than *kind of* merciful. And, fortunately, life is often funny.

The practice of the present moment

Each moment is all we need, not more.
MOTHER TERESA

I t was 1984—and something would change in me forever.

All I was doing was knocking the mud off my old, beat-up soccer shoes. In those days I was playing a lot of sports and had just finished some drills all by myself on the field behind church. Because I was in a league with a lot of players better than me, I did extra work to be competitive.

As I held those soccer shoes in my hands on that pretty October evening, the most amazing thing happened. Nothing. I mean nothing *around* me. But something *in* me changed deeply. It was as if I woke up for a moment. Suddenly I was fully present in the now. As I looked up, I saw clearly the gorgeous colors of the sunset. I smelled the mud from my cleats and felt the cool breeze on my face. And, instead of thinking ahead to what was next, or about something in the past, I was awake to that very moment. Over thirty years later, all of that remains quite vivid in my senses.

It was for me what some folks in Ireland refer to as a "thin place"—a place where the veil between this world and the next world is very thin. Normally, there seems to be something that separates what we see as we walk through our days, and the life beyond what we can see. But that evening I woke up to a thin place. For a moment I saw how close the other world really was and how deeply I was already connected to that world even here.

Over the years I've had other experiences of thin places. What I have now come to realize is this: If I walked through life as awake as I am meant to be, I could see that *every* moment is a thin place.

The way Jesus describes it: "The kingdom of God is at hand." Now. Not someday. Not some place "out there." The kingdom of God is always at hand, waiting to be birthed now, in just and loving goodness, in the quiet of our own hearts.

Even in the tough times: when you or I have been mistreated, lied about, or excluded, there is amazing love just on the other side of what we can see. In the midst of all that swirls inside us, with God's help it is possible to wake up a bit to see that the moment holds what we need and that deep down we are safe.

There is no reason to let ourselves be weighed down with the burden of bitterness when all the love in the universe is with us each moment.

Several months after those few seconds with my soccer cleats in hand, I visited one of our teenagers who had landed in jail. She asked if I could bring her the words from a poster that we had at our youth group meetings. She kept these words in her jail cell the entire time and says she has kept them with her since then as well. The poster simply read:

> I was regretting the past and fearing the future.
> Suddenly my God was speaking: "My name is I
> Am." God paused. I waited.
> God continued, "When you live in the past, with
> its mistakes and regrets, it is hard. I am not there.
> My name is not I WAS.
> When you live in the future, with its problems
> and fears, it is hard. I am not there. My name is not
> I WILL BE.
> When you live in this moment, it is not hard. I
> am here. My name is I AM."

For those who see, even a jail cell can be a thin place.

You and I? We are called by Jesus not to live in the past with regret or fury, nor to live in the future with anxiety or dread, but to continue to do the work to be awake to the kingdom of God, which is at hand.

The kingdom of God is *always* at hand, waiting for us to become awake to it that we might again see what is most real. In moments of anger or heartache, in times of laughter and love, when racing here or there or cleaning the mud off of soccer shoes, the kingdom of God is at hand.

May God give us the grace to realize more and more that every moment, every place, is a thin place. Even *this* very moment right now.

Will we see it too late?

Every saint has a past and
every sinner a future.

Perhaps you have heard of, or read, the classic book *All Quiet on the Western Front*. My critique? It offers a unique and important perspective for all of us. The novel follows the experience of a nineteen-year-old German soldier in World War I. His name is Paul. At one point the frightened young soldier is hiding in a shell hole. When an enemy soldier jumps into the same hole to hide, Paul instinctively pulls out his dagger and stabs him. The soldier dies shortly after that.

Paul, deeply troubled, looks in the soldier's pocket and discovers that the man's name was Gerald Duval, that he was a printer and obviously poor. This man who had been an abstraction, an enemy soldier, now becomes all too real for him. He finds a picture of a woman and a child. Moved, he speaks to the dead man: "Now, for the first time, I see you are a man like me....I see your wife and your face and our fellowship. Forgive me, comrade.

We always see it too late. Why do they never tell us that you are poor like us, that your mothers are just as anxious as ours, and that we have the same fear of death, and the same agony? Forgive me."

He saw it too late. Gerald was no different from him, but Paul had been taught—as had Gerald—that they should see each other only as enemies, not as a persons.

It is a danger for each of us that we will see it too late. It is easy to see others as merely statistics, even worse, as enemies—to forget that we are more alike than different. While it is important not to justify the misdeeds of others, it is also important not to think that everything that is wrong with this world is because of those people "out there."

This lack of seeing allows the many "isms" that we let divide us. This lack of seeing has allowed such tragedies as the Holocaust. This same lack of seeing can also keep us from doing the essential work of forgiveness.

One of my priest mentors, a wonderful man, talked about one of the benefits of hearing confessions in the Sacrament of Reconciliation. He said, "It helps me realize I am every person. There is a little of me in the sins of each of the people who come to me in sorrow." Personally, I find it humbling to hear confessions for that same reason.

When Jesus says we are to love our neighbors as ourselves, what if he did not mean "as much as" ourselves but because they *are* ourselves? We are one in God. Jesus' lifework could be described as having done everything he possibly could in his every moment to help us not see that too late.

Once, at the end of one of our parish retreats, we asked if any participants wanted to say a word or phrase about the blessing they found on the weekend. One of the men, a former basketball player and now coach, said: "I learned that behind every face is a story."

Forgiveness does not mean we throw away our ability to think critically. Nor do we stop the work of detachment and boundaries when they are needed. It's just that we are called to remember that we are more profoundly "in this together" than we usually can know.

In other words, can we remember that, if we checked the wallets of the people we think are so different from us, we would see pictures of their spouses and kids and parents?

May God help us not see it too late.

Learning to give an MRI

*Assumptions are unopened windows that
foolish birds fly into, and their broken bodies
are evidence gathered too late.*

BRYAN DAVIS

B ecause I played as many sports as I did, and
because I would sometimes get a bit banged up
along the way, I've had a few more MRIs than
most people. MRIs involve the use of *Magnetic Resonance
Imagers*, massive machines with powerful magnets that
unlock the secrets of the brain and the body. MRIs give
a picture of what is inside someone in a way that doctors
had previously only been able to see by surgically opening up a patient.

Recently I heard of a different type of MRI. This one
also reveals what is inside a person but is not solely the
realm of doctors and skilled technicians. For some who
do team building and leadership training activities, MRI
stands for the *Most Respectful Interpretation*. If a person
is crabby at work, instead of presuming that they are an
enemy or some kind of awful person, an MRI presumes

the best, and maybe even begins a conversation to discover what is going on in that person's life.

When was the last time *you* performed an MRI? Clearly Jesus counts on us to offer them.

Perhaps you know how aggravating it can be when someone does *not* offer you an MRI. Once I was making my way over to church on a Saturday afternoon for Confession when a young man screeched his car to a stop, jumped out, and ran into my arms sobbing. His sister had just been killed in a car wreck. We talked, I said a prayer with him, and I promised I would cancel an appointment so that as soon as Confession and Mass were over I could come to be with him and his family.

By the time I got to my confessional, I was five minutes late. A man whom I did not recognize was waiting. He exaggeratedly tapped on his watch several times and hissed, "This is a sacrament, you know."

By the grace of God I did not say the first thing I wanted to say. Thankfully, neither did I say the second or the third. Though I sometimes still feel a bit of a flash of anger when I think about that moment, I decided that day that I would try to recommit myself to try not do to others what he had done to me.

The vision that Jesus holds out for us, as difficult as it may be to achieve, is a world where the first response and the second and the third is always compassion, always to begin with an "MRI." Multiple times and in many ways he tells us, "Do not judge."

Yes, we can judge people's *actions*. We must use our

ability for critical thinking. People's lives can depend on that judgment. But when it comes to their *hearts*, we need to remember that we never have enough evidence to judge a person's heart, that the truth is often complicated, and that everyone hurts.

Dietrich Bonhoeffer, who was executed for rejecting Nazism, put it this way: "We must learn to regard people less in the light of what they do or don't do, and more in light of what they suffer."

For me, when I remember that, it usually helps me take things less personally, and I am less likely to give a knee-jerk response in anger. Sometimes I am even able to connect—at least internally—with the very one who just hurt or offended me in some way. For we all suffer.

There will always be people with whom we find ourselves wanting to respond in anger. Without justifying their behavior, it would serve us well to offer them an MRI. After the example of—and at the command of—Jesus, let us strive to remember that there is a good chance that that person is in great pain right now, that we don't know their story, and that if we did, it might just change everything.

A different good...

All is changed, changed utterly.
A terrible beauty is born.
W.B. YEATS

Michelle was new to our parish and full of life. She also suffered from lupus and its occasional flare-ups. At the age of twenty-four, this energetic and athletic young woman went in for surgery to lessen the inflammation in her back. Something went wrong, and Michelle came out paralyzed for life. The news was crushing. Our church family loved her the best we could through it all.

Some months later Michelle joined us for a parish retreat. At the end of the retreat, participants were invited to say anything they wanted to say to the others. Michelle asked for the microphone. From her wheelchair, Michelle looked up at everyone and said softly, "In the love I've found in all of you I have learned that I don't have to have two legs to walk with Jesus."

Michelle had come to know a great truth. She was not defined by what had happened to her. Life is often unfair. Sometimes life is so difficult we wonder how we could ever go on, or maybe why we would even want to. But there is something in us that nothing and no one can take from us. There is a power in the human spirit that can not only survive but grow stronger through what we have suffered.

Michelle was heartbroken to never again be able to walk or ski or do so many of the things she used to do. Yet Michelle told many a person that she learned so much through what she suffered, that she is now more alive and aware of what matters than she ever had been.

Our faith does not tell us that people will be kept free of suffering or protected from being treated unfairly. We *are* called to believe that—no matter what life throws at us—all the love in the universe remains present to us! What we most deeply need is always there.

It has been said that sometimes when you have to give up the life you planned, you find the new life that is waiting for you. Our job is to yield to the new life that God would like to birth from our heartache, to open ourselves so that God can lead us to a new and even deeper life.

Eventually I said goodbye to the parish that Michelle and I shared, and I did not see her again. Several years later, I was listening to a news story on the local radio station about a group of people picketing in the city for curb-cuts to make the streets and sidewalks of St. Louis safer for people in wheelchairs.

Suddenly, I realized that I knew the group's spokesperson, who was being interviewed. It was Michelle. Michelle made an insightful and heartfelt plea for the city to provide greater access for everyone with any form of disability or physical challenge. As I listened to her, I smiled deep inside and said quietly to myself, "Way to go, Michelle. You were right. You don't need two legs to walk with Jesus."

I choose joy

*If you have no joy, there's a leak
in your Christianity somewhere.*
BILLY SUNDAY

One Friday afternoon I saw something I will never forget. Our school community had gathered to do the "ice-bucket" challenge in solidarity with a parishioner named Joan who had ALS, commonly called "Lou Gehrig's Disease." Together we would pray for all who struggle with this awful disease. Soon the teachers, the principal, and the pastor would have buckets of ice water dumped on our heads. But before any of those things happened, Joan was first invited to the microphone. Joan had already lost her voice, so she held her tablet close to the microphone, and with a computer-generated voice, spoke a beautiful message of thanks and encouragement to all of us.

As her message played for us to hear, I looked first to her eyes and then to the eyes of her loving husband, Tom, who was standing off to the side. In Joan's eyes, I saw a certain vulnerability that I didn't usually see. Joan knew that losing her voice was but one of the many losses she faced. At the same time, in those eyes I saw the determined, spunky part of her that said, "This disease does not define me"—words I once heard her say out loud.

In the eyes of her husband, Tom, I saw great devotion to his wife, I saw deep sorrow, and I saw the price of love.

It was hard for me not to sob. I was not the only one for whom that was true.

A few days later I received a note from Joan. She thanked us for the support she had received, and then spoke of how she was choosing to cherish the simple things. When she would get sad, she said she chose not to focus on what she could no longer do but to focus on what she still *could* do.

Then she said: "When it hurts so much that my youngest granddaughter will never know my voice, I choose to be thankful that I can smile at her, hug her, hold her. I have to be happy with that now." Then she added, "My mantra at this time in my life is: 'Today, I choose joy.' That's what makes me happy. I choose joy."

You and me? We are free to make that same choice... or not.

Yes, suffering visits each of us. Life is unfair, people can be mean, and heartaches will come. We will pay a price when we try to remain loving and true. Of course, we will sometimes get angry and discouraged. We will get frightened and frustrated and feel all the feelings that Jesus himself felt.

But in the end, a joy-filled life is a decision. Do we choose joy or not? No one else can make that choice for us.

Nor is it a one-time choice. Choosing joy is a life-stance that needs to be nurtured. If I want to find stuff to complain about and be unhappy about, it is there. There is always plenty to be crabby about. If I want to find things for which to be grateful, there are even more of those. It's true. There are so incredibly many more reasons to be thankful than not. But I need to choose to focus on those or I won't see them. The more I look for things for which to be grateful, the more I find them. For they are everywhere and always.

God wants me to have a joy-filled, hope-filled, and meaning-filled life. And God will help that happen in more ways than I could ever know. But there is that which God will not do. In the end, God cannot choose for me.

How tragic it would be if I wasted my life on hatred instead of doing the difficult work of forgiving. Any time I spend trying to choose joy over bitterness, hope over hate, and thankfulness over resentment is truly choosing life over death. With all my heart I believe it is worth it.

Thank you for being generous enough to read this. Though I don't even know who you are, I do know that there is a deep-down goodness in you. You can trust that I will pray for you, for I will. Please, if you would, whisper a prayer for me as well. May God help us be people who dare to forgive.

APPENDIX

No one can take away your dignity

I thought such awful thoughts that
I cannot even say them out loud because
they would make Jesus want to drink
gin straight out of the cat dish.

ANNE LAMOTT

Too many have suffered too terribly at the hands of others through physical or sexual abuse. The harm is immeasurable. Yet, there is a dignity in the human spirit that no one can take from us.

Although the prayer below has the rhyme and meter of a child's prayer, I offer it for people of every age (and perhaps for the child in each person who has ever survived abuse). It's called: "I Have Great Worth and Goodness." It comes with my gut-felt heartache for all who have suffered abuse at the hands of another. It also comes with my deep admiration for your goodness and your spirit, which were in no way diminished by what was done to you.

I Have Great Worth and Goodness
AN ABUSE SURVIVOR'S PRAYER

When someone has been wronged, Dear God,
It must make You so sad.
You never want us to be harmed
Or made to think we're bad.

Sometimes I feel mixed-up inside,
Though I did nothing wrong.
Please help me not to blame myself
Or think I don't belong.

YOU think that I am precious, God,
I'm always in your heart.
No matter what is said or done
We never are apart.

 My goodness is not lessened
By what was done to me.
I have great worth and beauty, God,
A loving dignity.

Please help me to begin again
And grow to be more free.
Help me know I'm loved and good,
That You believe in me.

You are more than your sin

*Whatever God does, the first outburst
is always compassion.*
ECKHART

O ne of my siblings once told me a story about a young man who was caught shoplifting. The kid's dad drove across town to bail out his son. It was a quiet car ride home. Finally, the dad spoke. "Son, if you ever want something that badly in your life that you'd steal for it again, let your mother or I know. We will work longer hours; we'll sacrifice for it. Let us buy it for you."

Instead of shaming his son, this dad generously offered mercy and kindness. This young man would never forget that moment. His dad had given him a glimpse of the mercy and kindness that is at the heart of God.

That mercy and kindness is for *each* of us and for *all* of God's children.

You and I—and all God's people—are each a mix of saint and sinner. We are in trouble if we deny either part of that. Perhaps we sometimes don't see the reality and the consequences of our sin and its harm on the world. At other times, our temptation is to over-identify with our sin. Maybe there are those who never let us live down our past mistakes. Some act as if our worst moment defines us. No: you and I are so much more than our sin.

Even if you did not hear this growing up, I am convinced God would say to you: "Deep down you are good; you are wanted; you are loved for yourself as you are. In my heart, you are safe. You are more than your sin."

To help that be more real, I invite you to use your imagination for a short experience of prayer.

Though some use imagination more readily than others, I encourage you to try it.

For prayer, I always think it is good to find a posture that helps us be both comfortable and alert, and I encourage you to place yourself in that posture at this time. Please do not be limited by what I suggest. If your imagination takes you elsewhere, relax into that. At one point I will suggest words that God might have for you. Please listen for what God has for you through those words, or in spite of them. If it helps to have music in the background and/or someone else slowly read the words while you listen, I encourage that.

When using imagination in prayer, some find it helps to first take a few deep breaths. You might do that now.

As you do so, become aware of having a body...of being alive...of being you.

In your imagination I invite you to think of something about yourself—past or present—of which you are not so proud.

Perhaps in your gut, just below the level of your regular thinking, there are a few things about yourself and your history that eat at you. Maybe it's something you're embarrassed about. Perhaps you feel shame at some sinful pattern. Maybe you hurt someone you truly love. Perhaps you've said you're sorry many times. Perhaps you've never told anyone.

It doesn't have to be the worst thing. But if there was something that you wish you had never done or a way that you behave that you wish you didn't, what would that be? Without fear or shame, try to name that to yourself.

Now, I invite you to bring that to God in any way you would like. Either with gesture, words, or just by your awareness, open up to God something for which you are sorry.

After you have done so, and when you are ready, listen to God's response.

First, let God speak your name. God continues: "I know you. I know who you are, where you've been, what you've done. And I love you. You are so much more than any mistake or sin. I see your deep-down goodness. You never had enough power to make me stop loving you. You don't now. Please, go forward now, not back in shame. Just go love this world. I love you now...and I will love you forever."

Now again become aware of being in the place you are. As you do so, try to keep a sense of the presence of God with you.

Again, some people find it easier than others to use their imagination in this way. If that was helpful for you, I'm glad. If not, or you fell asleep, that's okay. It is still true that you are more than your sin. And you and I have a God who is filled with love for us, a love that truly never ends.

You could loosen your grip. You could start to let go.

A GUIDED PRAYER EXPERIENCE

Be kind whenever possible. It is always possible.
DALAI LAMA

Some years ago, a man described an interesting experience he had with his three children. The kids had had a fairly intense argument one night. At two in the morning they were awakened by a severe storm and the sound of tornado sirens. Dad ran upstairs, didn't see them, and yelled, "Where are you?" A little voice answered, "We are all in the closet forgiving each other."

For all the reasons described earlier in this book, there is wisdom in choosing to do the work of forgiveness *before* we are afraid we will die.

While not excusing the bad behavior of others, why let ourselves become bitter? What good do we do to carry hatred in response? Though the work of forgiveness is difficult, we do not have to do it all by ourselves. There are ways to be wounded yet continue to enjoy the goodness and beauty of our life's journey in the days we have been given.

Perhaps some version of this little prayer activity might be of help.

As with the previous guided reflection, I encourage you to find a posture that helps you be both comfortable and alert. During this meditation I will suggest a dialogue you might have with God or to use as a starting point for wherever you feel led. If it helps you to have music in the background and/or someone else slowly read the words while you listen, please do so.

First I encourage a few deep breaths. As you deeply breathe in and out, become aware of having a body...of being alive...of being you.

In your imagination, I invite you to think of something that makes you angry even now when you think of it. What is some way you were treated poorly? It doesn't have to be the worst thing. But where do you find some anger inside yourself these days?

In your imagination, take some time to prepare to bring that to God. What would you want to say to God about that?

Now, with or without words, tell God what is on your heart about this hurt.

After you have done so, perhaps you could imagine a conversation with God that goes something like this:

You: It was so unfair, God.

God: It was.

You: God, what happened to me was not okay.

God: No, it was not. It hurts me that you suffered what you did.

You: I know we are called to forgive, but I don't know. It's hard, God.

God: I understand.

      (*pause*)

God: Do you want to let it go?

You: Part of me does; part of me doesn't.

      (*silence*)

You: I don't know if I can do this.

God: You don't have to do it by yourself.

      (*silence*)

God: You could give it to me. Would it be good if I helped you carry it?

      (*silence*)

God: You decide what you want to do. I will wait.

       (*silence*)

You: Here, God, here it is. As best as I can,
       I give this to you.

God: I will carry this too. When it hurts again,
       offer it to me anew.

You: I will try.

God: I will go with you to help you. Always,
       always, always I will be with you.

When you are ready, please again become aware of being
in the place you are, and try to keep a sense of the presence of God with you as you do so.

Of course, some people find it easier than others to
use their imagination in this way. If that was helpful for
you, I'm glad. If not, that's okay. It is still true that you
and I do not need to do the work of letting go of our
hurts all by ourselves. We have a God who has promised
to go with us, a God who will help carry the burden with
us and for us. With God's help we *can* loosen our grip a
bit on our hurts and angers.

We are in this together

A PRAYER RITUAL FOR FAMILIES, FRIENDS, AND COMPANIONS

All the darkness in the world cannot extinguish the light of a single candle.

One day, the first grade teacher was called into the hall by the principal to meet a new student for her class. The young boy had been born with only one arm. The teacher knew that kids can be pretty direct, sometimes, and worried that one of the other students might say something that embarrassed the boy. She wished she would have had time to remind her students that it's good that we all look different on the outside and that, on the inside, we are all much more alike than different. We are *each* special children of God. But there was no time for that. So she just whispered a prayer that it would all go well, and it did.

There is an old rhyme you might know that involves putting our hands together and demonstrating the words: "Here's the church, here's the steeple, open the door, and here's all the people." The teacher decided to use that rhyme to end the day. But as soon as she began she realized that she had herself put the young boy in an awkward position. She looked up just in time to see the little girl in the row next to him reach up with her hand and say: "Here, we can make church together." And so she put her hand to his, and together they did just that.

We are each like those children. We each have something to offer; we are each incomplete in ourselves. Together we make church.

This little prayer service might be helpful for family members, friends, participants in a faith-sharing group, or others who are called to work side by side. For there is no way to live or work closely together without sometimes getting on each other's nerves or hurting one another. The work of forgiveness helps us be who we are meant to be for one another.

Family members or friends gather around an unlit candle or other symbol. The person who takes the part of the leader either composes their own prayer or says something similar to the following:

Merciful God, we are sinners who need you.
Your great love shines as light in our darkness.

(If you are using a candle, light the candle now)

One at a time participants read the following prayers:

> » Fill the darkness in our world with the light of
> your peace.
> » Fill the darkness in our homes with the light of
> forgiveness.
> » Fill the darkness in our hearts with the light of
> your love.

The candle is then passed to each person individually, with the person holding the candle asking forgiveness of the others by saying:

I am sorry for _____.
(give general areas or specific examples)

—AND/OR—

For any ways I have not loved you
as well as you deserved, I am sorry.

After each person has taken their turn, there is a moment for anyone to add anything else they would like to say. Then all join hands and pray the Lord's Prayer together. To end, the leader invites all to offer and receive a sign of peace.

Do I *have* to forgive? How?

A THOUGHT FOR CHILDREN

In a world where you can be anything, be kind.

ETTA TURNER

Grown-ups are not the only ones who wrestle with questions about forgiveness. There is a wonderful little booklet called *Living Faith KIDS* for children. Each quarter I have been writing a short column called "Ask Fr. Joe" in which I respond to the questions of children. Below are two of their questions and my responses. May God help us encourage—and model—the crucial work of forgiveness for our children.

Dear Fr. Joe,
Do I HAVE to forgive my enemies?
» *Jackson*

Dear Jackson,

Certainly, no one and no thing can make you forgive. So, to answer your question, no, you don't HAVE to forgive. But I have a different question. Are you open to the idea that it might possibly be worth it?

Before you answer that, please understand that to forgive does NOT mean you are saying it is okay if someone is mean, hateful, or unfair. And, no, you don't need to let anyone keep hurting you. Please do what you can to be safe.

Of course, after we have been hurt, it's often not easy to shake our anger. To be brave enough to try to forgive is hard work. But if we don't do that work, whether we are aware of it or not, something inside us becomes less alive.

No matter how badly someone treated us, it is really important that we don't become hateful in return. It is *never* worth it to be mean.

Instead, Jackson, I pray you won't give away your power to stay loving and true. Think of Jesus, the best person who ever lived. People lied about Jesus, hurt him, and even killed him. But Jesus never became mean in return. Jesus continued to be the best and most loving person that ever lived. He forgave people who hurt him and was the most alive and free and truly happy person ever!

So, to your question, do you HAVE to forgive

your enemies, the answer is, "It depends." It depends on whether or not you want to be truly happy like Jesus was.

In Christ,
Fr. Joe

Dear Father Joe,
A drunk driver killed my cousin.
How am I supposed to forgive him?
» *Thomas*

Dear Thomas,

First, of all, Thomas, I am so sorry for your family's heartache. The death of your cousin is such a senseless loss.

You asked how you are supposed to forgive the drunk driver that killed your cousin. First, please know that to forgive does not mean to act like no wrong was done. That someone would drive while drunk is wrong.

But you are wise to work on forgiving, or else you let that drunk driver claim another victim: *you*. When we carry a grudge, something *in us* dies. To *not* forgive is like drinking rat poison and then waiting for the rat to die. Maybe the rat will suffer in some way, maybe not. But certainly *we* will. We might think that it will be easier if we get revenge first. It will not. There is no life in revenge.

For most of us, forgiveness is a three-step process. First, we freely choose to forgive and to let go of our desire for revenge. Second, we ask God to help us let it go. And third, because the anger and hurt will come back, we do steps one and two again and again.

It is such important work. Forgiveness is at the heart of the gospel…and the heart of a truly holy and happy life. You and your family will be in my heart and prayers.

In Christ,
Fr. Joe